Me, G, and the Locust Tree

BY CLAY ANDERSON ILLUSTRATED BY ELIE NURYANTI

ISBN 978-1-7322418-3-1

Copyright © 2018 Clay Anderson

All rights reserved. No part of this publication may be reproduced, distributed, or transmitted in any form or by any means, including photocopying, recording, or other electronic or mechanical methods, without the prior written permission of the author, except in the case of brief quotations embodied in critical reviews and certain other noncommercial uses permitted by copyright law. For permission requests, write to the author at author@clayanderson.com.

First Printing, 2018

Discounts are available for quantity purchases, and for schools or associations.
For ordering information, visit:
http://www.clayanderson.com

Illustrations by Elie Nuryanti
https://www.fiverr.com/elienuryanti

Printed in China

For Garrett.

Swing for the sky.
I love you, today and always.

I used to be a kid.

And when I was a kid, this is the house where I grew up.

I had a favorite climbing tree:
 the maple in the front yard.

I loved that tree.
　　I spent hours in that tree.

One day the tree was a castle.

The next it was a spaceship.

And the day after that, it was full of friends.

I could see the tree from my bedroom window.

When a big storm blew in,
I would watch it get whipped by the wind.
I always worried a strong gust would knock it down.

But I never worried about our other trees.

See this locust tree?
It has been there as long as I can remember.
It's a good, strong tree.

But it has never meant much to me.
Because it was never *my* tree.

I'm not a kid anymore. I'm a dad now.
And this is my son, Garrett.

My little G.

But G doesn't worry about the maple tree like I did, because the maple tree is no longer there.

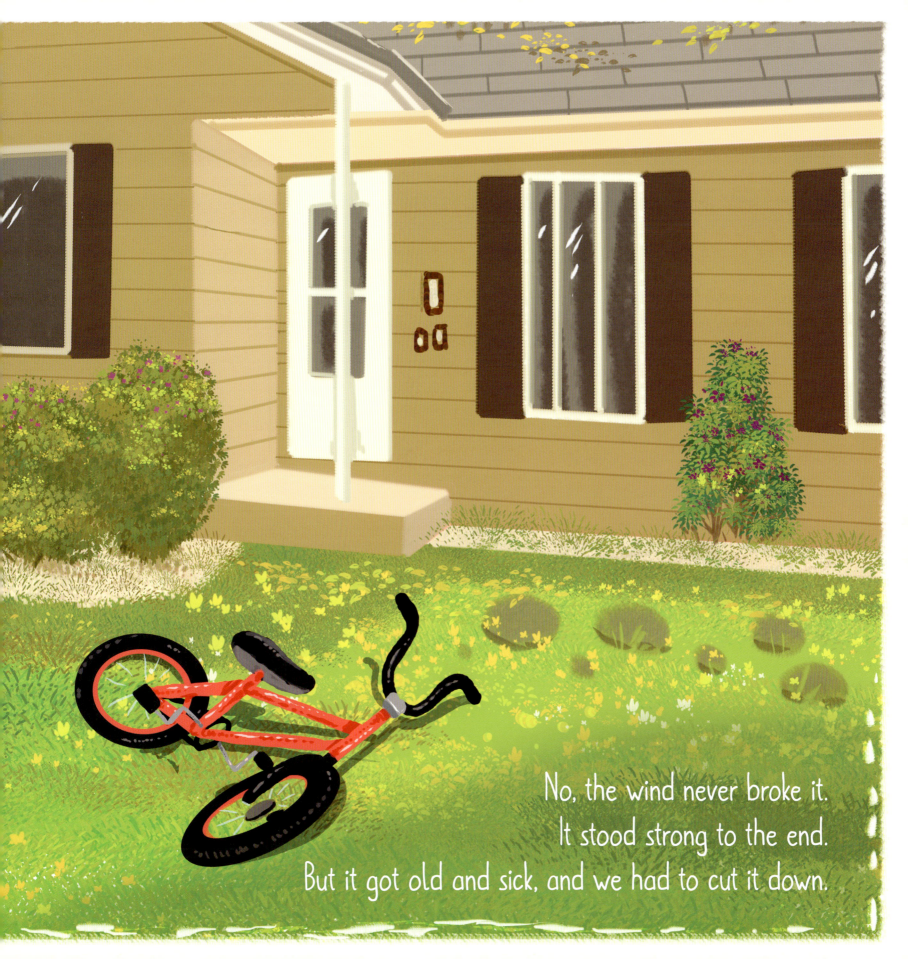

But that locust tree? It's still there. Still good. Still strong.

Last summer, I wanted to hang a swing for G and his brother and sisters.

And the best place to hang it was from a branch high in the locust tree.

So now, the locust tree gets to do something more than just be a tree.
He gets to hold giggling, singing, swinging children.

And he loves it.

How do I know?

Well, this may sound odd,
but I struck up a conversation with him the other day.

The locust tree is more than fifty years old, even older than I am.
But he told me he's having the time of his life.

And he told me something else.

"This won't last forever," he said.

"What do you mean?" I asked.

"I remember when you were a boy,"
said the locust tree.

"You would spend hours in the maple.
That tree loved it as much as you did.
He loved when you climbed, and explored, and imagined.

I always wished I could be like that maple tree."

"And now I get to bring joy to your kids.

They can't wait to see me.
I get to hold them in my branches.
Play with them.
Swing them until they burst out laughing!"

"But they'll get bigger.

And older.

And they won't want to swing.

At least, not every day."

"G will come back to visit.
There will be a twinkle in his eye, and a smile on his face.
He'll climb on the swing, and remember these days.

But these days will be a memory.
And like the maple, I'll go back to just being a tree.

And that's okay."

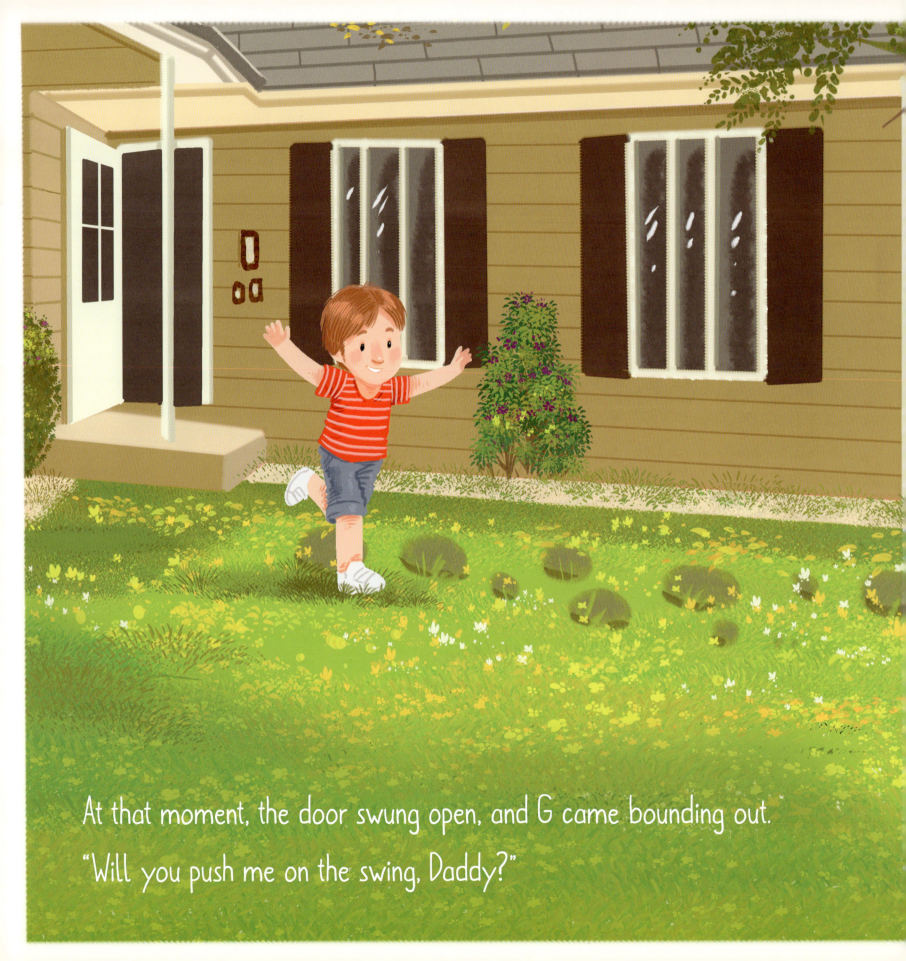

At that moment, the door swung open, and G came bounding out.

"Will you push me on the swing, Daddy?"

"Of course I will, Garrett."

The locust tree rustled its leaves in joy.
Because the tree and me, we're going to cherish every moment...

...while it lasts.